MY TALK

## MY TALK

Ah what a life Lovey and I am still talking to you. I know I have to stop writing soon because this phase of life is almost over; thus I am listening to Natural Mystic by Robert Nesta Marley.

Lovey this man foretold and told and no one could over stand and or comprehend him; his music.

Wow.

So Lovey; Black Death is that tall and brown; wide.

Lovey am I correct, but why did I see a Black Jesus that is brown in hue?

Are you trying to tell me that Black Death is now going to die?

He was a giant; tall and wide and he was lying on his back as if in a dead and or sleeping state. I cannot fully remember the dream if in fact it was a dream.

Nice brown skin but I truly did not see his face. But Lovey really? Does this mean all death on land and sea will soon be over and you are going to reclaim earth as your own once again?

Are humans finally going to get the truth of life from these books as well as the songs of truth by Robert Nesta Marley (Bob Marley)?

Are they going to get the full truth from Marcus Mosiah Garvey and reclaim their heritage and truths; You?

Lovey, I know what you are saying in regards to me. I know that once we separate I will not find you again. But Lovey, do I truly have you?

Yes I know you are saying I have you, but do I truly have you?

Am I not confused by you?
Am I not left shackled and chained by you?
Do I not feel as if I am in a never ending maze with you?

So how can I lose someone or something I truly do not have?

Do I not question you and question your authority?
Do I not tell you that you are wrong?

So if I do all these things and you have not lashed out at me, are you saying you are truly pleased with me?

Are you saying you have no complaints when it comes to me and my dealings with you?

I know you keep telling me if I lose you I will be lost, but I ask you, if we get dirty water to drink, will our spirit and or soul including self; body not be dirty; become dirty?

No one can or will become clean if the waters of life are dirty. We will forever be dirty; confused.

You cannot come clean because you're drinking and bathing in dirty water. Thus your spirit will forever remain dirty and you Lovey know this.

## <u>So tell me now, how can we as humans say we are clean if all we consume and drink is filthy and unclean; dirty?</u>

Thus TIME WILL TELL by Robert Nesta Marley (Bob Marley). He did tell us the BABYLON SYSTEM is a vampire sucking the blood of the sufferers. He did plea with Babylon and the thieves they educated to tell the truth. **He too knew that TRUTH IS EVERLASTING LIFE; thus he told us to rebel against Babylon.** We have to rebel against Babylon Lovey. We need to know the truth and live by the truth if we truly want and need to live. We cannot continue to let the devil and their band of thieves teach and or educate us. It is not right Lovey, its wrong. Babylon is for

Babylonians; so why are you allowing your children and people to be indoctrinated and assimilated in their hellish communities and religion; evil systems?

Rebelling is not arms Lovey. We can rebel by walking away from Babylon. We will no longer walk around in circles on their press of slavery anymore.

**Babylon need to fall; thus let Babylon fall because BABYLON DID TAKE YOU FROM US.**

BABYLON GAVE US DIRTY FOOD TO EAT AND DIRTY WATER TO DRINK SO THAT WE CAN NEVER EVER COME HOME TO YOU. THEY ARE TAKING US TO HELL AND THIS PRACTICE MUST STOP.

Religion and Politics including our sins and the sins of our surroundings cannot take us to you. All they do is keep us from you and you know this. So what say you Lovey?

We cannot find you Lovey due to our unclean ways and nature. We have to come home clean to you because you are clean. No one dirty can come to you and say they are going to reside with you come on now. Even I know this.

YOU DO NOT LIKE DIRT LOVEY. So why are you keeping us dirty?

YOU ARE CLEAN AND WHEN WE ARE DIRTY YOU HAVE NOTHING TO DO WITH US BECAUSE WE STINK. Dirt is on us and me smell foul.

WE HAVE TO CLEAN UP SELF INCLUDING SPIRIT AND LIVE BY THE TRUTH BEFORE YOU WILL HAVE ANYTHING TO DO WITH US.

You and I know the truth. Now I am telling you to "**tell the children the true truth" so that they can live.** We can no longer trod under the confines and mazes of death and their people anymore. So truly release our people Lovey from the confines of hell. We need the truth and you have it to give so truly give it without end.

Now Lovey let's move to AMBUSH IN THE NIGHT by Robert Nesta Marley (Bob Marley). **LOVEY I DEDICATE THIS SONG TO EVERY BLACK NATION UNIVERSALLY AND GLOBALLY. THIS IS THEIR SONG FOR THEM (THE BLACK RACE GLOBALLY) TO OPEN THEIR EYES AND WAKE UP FROM THEIR DEAD STATE.**

See Lovey, we keep fighting for their (evils) nasty religions and customs and I truly don't know why. They belittle us, and instead of having some shame we continue on in their nasty societies.

We keep killing our self to be with them in hell; Thus HELL IS FULL OF BLACK PEOPLE and we truly don't know it.

We buy into their crap of lies and deceit and now when the truth comes; **_WE REFUSE TO ACCEPT THE TRUTH AND WALK AWAY FROM THEIR DEAD MAN SOCIETIES._**

We need to know the full truth Lovey.
I am not one of them Lovey, and will never be like my own Black Race because I do not buy into the crap of integration. Nor do I buy into the crap of lies they tell and feed us in their books of lies and deceit; death.

I know you and they can't tell me anything about you. Thus their assimilation techniques will never work because knowledge is not belief. So they can keep their wretched beliefs because beliefs cannot get me to you, only knowledge can. I don't think when it comes to you Lovey I know; know you.

I never belonged and I will never belong because your truth and spirit; life is engrained in me despite me telling you I want and need to leave you.

**_So Lovey, truly listen to this song because I REFUSE TO BE WHAT THEY WANT ME TO BE. I AM ME AND I HAVE TO BE ME._**

I CANNOT BE CONTROLLED BY THEM AND I WILL NOT LET THEM CONTROL ME AND LEAD ME TO HELL. If humanity needs conformity then coodles to them. I am not them. I am perfect and true for me and yes you even when you piss me off by your lack of listening ways.

But Lovey, why should I have to? Am I becoming soft when it comes to my father?

No, I heard the tiredness and anger in the voice of my brother. All is left on him and because I truly love him, I will help him (my brother). And no Lovey don't even think of it. I truly do not seek favour and or blessing from you for this. I need to help my biological own. He is tired and I have to step up to the plate and help him. Besides, I have my gorgeous mother already and that's good enough for me. Hey Lovey, I have you too; hence I kissed you on the cheek and I am smiling. Truly thank you for being with me and being you. You are my blessing and you will forever be. So not because I say I want to walk away from you should you walk away from me. Yu noa sey mi caane guh far from yu. But thank you for reminding me of you and our pledge; truth. Never stop doing this because yu noa sey mi a tyrant that is more than crazy for you.

So as I listen to AMBUSH IN THE NIGHT and dedicate this song to all blacks globally, truly open our eyes and ears including spirit and soul for us to learn the truth. Lovey, if you can block every way and ways of sin from stopping us to receive, learn and know the truth, please do so right away and or from now.

Lovey you know Death and their people are going to do all to stop me. So commission it everywhere in earth, under the earth, in the universe, under the universe and especially in the waters of earth and life, the trees of earth and life and the breeze of earth and life that no evil or good stop me from spreading and teaching the truth of you and life especially the black race for more than infinite and indefinite lifetimes and generations forever ever without end starting now, before December 2015 as of September 19 2015.

Lovey, truly do not change from me because I've told you dirty cannot become clean if we know not the truth. No one dirty can come to you because unclean do not have the truth and without the full truth we cannot come to you nor can we reside in you and with you.

You are life thus you are the key to good and true life. If we do not have this key; You, we are lost. You've been showing me this. *YOU SHOWED ME WITHOUT YOU WE ARE LOST; WE CANNOT FIND YOU NO MATTER HOW HARD WE SEARCH; LOOK.*

Humanity do not know this. SO NOW WE KNOW THAT WHEN WE LEAVE YOUR FOLD, WE ARE LOST AND CONFUSED; CANNOT FIND YOU.

_Thus it's not up to the clergy or anyone to clean you; it is up to us. We have to clean self and become clean before we can know you. You are not belief but knowledge. Belief changes but knowledge is secure; cannot change. So in all that we do, we have to secure our self and we have to become clean._

So in all that I do Lovey, thank you for being my hand luggage because you truly go everywhere with us and not just me. So as the stage is set for the destruction of humanity; we as humans cannot afford to lose you. We have to regain you. Thus we have to clean self and come back to you true; whole.

_Many things you've shown me and because of this, I now know how THE AIR, FLYING AND OR AIRPORTS ARE IMPORTANT TO YOU AND THE KNOWLEDGE YOU'VE GIVEN US; TEACH ME._

So as humans, we have to respect flight; the heavens above. And respect does not mean worship people because I know some of you are going to want to go out there and worship the air above and or the heavens.

Yes people will do this my true family. Just as how some people worship the dead, trees, cows and what have you; they will worship the air and or the heavens. Sad but true.

So my trule family, it's time for us to clean self. It's hard to do it by ourselves. So if we can congregate and meet in pure and true truth and honesty, we will clean each other together; meaning help each other in a positive and clean; true way.

**You are my true family. So if I can help you to ease your burden and pick you up when I can, I will be there. And if I COULD HELP CLEAN YOU SO THAT WE COULD WALK HAND IN HAND INTO TOMORROW I WOULD.**

Know that true life cannot end and when the flesh of man; you are gone; life still lives on for you if you are good and clean; true. So let's strive together for goodness and truth. If you can hold my hand, hold it because I refuse to lie to you, and I refuse to be a hypocrite. I do all to live by my truths thus know me.

I know trusting is hard because it took me a while to trust Lovey. I battle him until this day; hence you have these books to see; well prove my words.

Listen, I am not perfect in all. No I am. We all are perfect in what we do despite the wrongs that we do. Remember I told you about the lie in some of these books and how lies seem so true. ***Well know you and the lies of men; humans.*** I did. Thus I walk away from many and no one can come say Michelle you're my true friend and the world knows it.

Family, my true family. No human being can hold up their hand and say I am your true friend because I have none. My true friend is Lovey and My Mother and they are in the spiritual realm. I have no fleshy true friends because humans are not true, so I truly do not need any.

But a friend is a friend. A friend is just a friend to you but a true friend is truly rare. Listen to Stephen Marley's False Friend and tell me about friends. Thus I truly and wholeheartedly want no friends. Like I said, I have a true friend in Lovey and my gorgeous and beautiful mother. Fleshy people I have no need for when it comes to friendship because I have truth. Once you as my true family become true; clean, then we will become true friends that are truly truthful and honest; pure.

Does it get lonely?

Yes, but despite my writings and rants to Lovey, he is truly there for me because HE'S TEACHING ME ABOUT FLIGHT.

**WHEN HE TRULY WANTS AND NEED ME TO SEE THINGS AND KNOW THINGS, HE PUTS THEM IN THE BLUE AND WHITE SKY.**

**HE PUTS HIS WORDS ON PLACES LIKE SCHOOLS.**

**ASK QUESTIONS FOR ME TO ANSWER.**

All these could be you. You see the way he teaches and educates me and you are no different.

In all I do, I am hoping we; me and him (he and I) will prepare a good and true environment for all of you.

An environment that is void of all sin and evil.

I've learnt many things hence there are different levels of sin; thus the different levels of death that I am finding out now.

# THE RICH MAN'S SIN IS NOT LIKE THE POOR MAN'S SIN. HENCE THE GREY AND UGLINESS I AM SEEING.

The rich man's sin whether male or female is ugly to the point where you want to vomit when you see it, and I've mentioned about the vomit in the book fourteen of the MY TALK SERIES OF BOOKS.

The greyish skin tone is nasty and for me to see whites turning an ugly state of grey in the form of black people is horrible and disrespectful of and or to the colour black to me. But there is nothing I can do about it because this is what I saw and I cannot camouflage it for anyone. So some truly evil white people die as ugly and gross black people. No not die, I was seeing the spirit of these people not their death but eventual death.

Damn rich white people some of ya'll spirit is gross and ugly. Nasty to the point of making me want to vomit and that's gross; truly sad on your part.

I truly don't want to be any of you literally because you are ugly. You ugly. What's that cheer they do about ugly? Well you ugly. Sorry Lovey but I had to do that.

*THUS STOP HATING BASED ON HUE.*
*STOP HATING PERIOD BECAUSE YOU NOW KNOW THE UGLINESS OF YOUR SPIRIT.*

*STOP CALLING BLACK PEOPLE UGLY BECAUSE WE ARE NOT THE UGLY ONES; YOU ARE. YOUR SPIRIT IS LITERALLY UGLY BECAUSE OF YOUR SINS AND RACIST ATTITUDE; GREED AND RICHNESS.*

Oh fam, my true family. Tin foil and or aluminum foil without the shine is the best colour of grey that these ugly people's spirit looks like. Lovey teaches but you have to be willing to learn. We are his students and to get to him is a way; long way from here. ***THUS NO ONE CAN GO TO HIM AND OR GET TO HIM WITH A DIRTY AND UNCLEAN SPIRIT.***

We do not need people to speak for us because he did give us a voice to speak to him.

If you want to speak to him just come true and clean. Be honest to him and with him. Each step you take to him he takes 1 - 10 steps and more towards you.

I've told you in other books never lie to him.

Also, do not expect him to answer you right away. Give him time. For some of us, he does take years to answer us and this wait; waiting game will piss you royally off like me. It's as if he's not listening. Well you know me and the way I am in these books.

Learning, trusting and knowing is truly not easy for some of us. We want things done right away like me and it cannot happen. We cannot get things right away.

Why not you are saying?

Are we clean?

Do we not do things to piss off Lovey as well?

Is Lovey your god?

Listen, not because Lovey does not answer me right away does not mean he won't with you.

I have to write for him and when you are on his pathway, evil does try to hinder you in every way.

It's September 24, 2015 and I was talking to Lovey. I know he cannot fix everything in our lives because he did not sin for us; nor did he cause our lives to be filled with pain and heartache.

Our sins are our sins and we cannot look to him to fix everything for us. It's not fair to him. No, we can look to him to fix all because he is Lovey; God.

Can he fix all?

No, he cannot because we are not all his people.

## Evil have and has their race of people and good have theirs.

## <u>We as humans are the unbalanced ones that seek the favour of death when we cannot get what we want.</u>

Some people turn to secret societies for wealth and fame.

Some steal.

Some kill.

Some lie and deceive; cheat.

Some destroy their surroundings and environment.

All in all, we do not think of the consequences of our actions. <u>**And it's only when things go awry we are looking to Lovey to fix the mess we've caused.**</u>

DURING THE GOOD TIMES WE DON'T KNOW LOVEY, BUT AS SOON AS THINGS HEAT UP AND GO BAD; WE ARE RUNNING TO HIM SAYING, SO AND SO IS NOT FAIR, THEY ARE EVIL AND YOU NEED TO HELP ME. I CANNOT TAKE THAT PERSON ANYMORE. LOOK HOW HARD I WORK AND THIS; THIS IS WHAT'S BEFALLING ME. GOD YOU ARE UNFAIR. DO I NOT GO TO CHURCH AND PRAISE YOU?

DO I NOT WORSHIP YOU?

DO I NOT DO MY BEST FOR YOU?

SO WHY ARE YOU LETTING THIS EVIL BEFALL ME; HAPPEN TO ME?

I DID NOT CAUSE THIS ON MYSELF BUT YET YOU ARE ALLOWING THIS EVIL TO HINDER ME?

WHY?

But in all of our fuming, we forgot that we were the ones to miss his warning signs. So how can he fix our messes when we are the ones to willingly and wilfully create these messes? We are the ones that are not listening to his good counsel.

You see how he's trying with me when it comes to my homeland. Yes I want to go back and told him I am going to go back. My homeland is the only land I can afford. I did make arrangements to go back home but have to put it off until 2016. It's not that I want to disappoint him, but I need to leave this land I am in and he's truly not listening. I want and need out with every fabric of my being; truth, and he keeps me here.

I am truly not happy here.

Maybe it's the province I am in, but I am truly not happy here. My spirit and life yearns, no, not yearns, but craves nature; the trees and waterways and where I am I truly do not have this. ___I don't know people but I cannot wait on him Lovey for a good shower of rain; prosperity.___ I have to build a good and true foundation for me.

Yes disobedience is a sin and it is death. But what do you do when the one you truly love is distant; away from you; not listening to you? How do you go on with him knowing that he is failing you thus you are failing him?

There is only so much that I can do because my spirit and or our spirit is the driving force in our lives. You want and need to live clean, but if the one you look to for more than guidance and cleanliness is truly not guiding you on the right path, what do you do?

Is he or she not telling you indirectly that they don't care?

Is this not what Lovey is doing to me in a way? Is he not telling me he does not care in human context not spiritual context?

Yes he's shown me if I leave him I will not be able to find him, but have I truly found him?

Is this not a game on his part to keep me burrowed and confused; locked in his world of unhappiness and loneliness?

So in all that you do and have, you have to think of you and your sanity and walk away. I have to think of my sanity and happiness and walk away. It's not fair for anyone to be hindered when it comes to true goodness of self and others; life. It's not fair for anyone to live in a world of unhappiness and lies. This Lovey cannot see. He knows the truth, but what good is knowing the truth if the truth is kept muzzled and or under lock and key?

When you do this, you are hindering the progress of the person you claim to love so. Thus loving so is truly not loving true nor is loving so real in my book. Hey maybe this is a test on Lovey's part to see how far he can push me before I leave him; go?

Listen, as individuals some of us do give true and love true. No, I will not go there. If we as humans loved true and were honest with each other and Lovey himself; we would not be in this mess here on earth. Therefore, as humans we are not fair in our ways and judgment. I too am not fair with Lovey at times. Maybe I am expecting too much when it comes to him. He is Lovey and he should be able to fix things in my life right away. Certain things should not befall me. I've made him Lovey my good and true foundation and framework of life; so nothing should hinder my progress and prosperity; goodness of life. Come on now. Impenetrable foundations and frameworks is what I need from Lovey so that evil will never ever befall me or hinder me ever again, and he cannot give me this. Listen, Lovey knows how I feel about him when it comes to my true love of him. He is my right thus I put all my truth and true love in him.

<u>I know I am lost without him hence on this day JOHNNY GILL'S IT WOULD BE YOU say it best for me. If I do not have Lovey I would die. We all would die because he is our saving grace in life and in all that we do. Thus we have to wake up and stop living as the dead.</u>

I am so going to jump ahead and interrupt this book and or the flow of this book. As black people Lovey has tried with us based on hue and deeds. Yes I am bringing hue, no forget it I refuse to base anything on hue because some whites are blacks and they do fall under the banner of black. As humans we do not see our need and dependence when it comes to Lovey. We all need him but billions have and has turned from him and accepted other gods of nastiness. This is why he's left us and cannot be found.

We do not respect him nor are we true to him.

WITH ME SEEING ZION FALL AND WITH ME SEEING ZION'S TIME EXPIRE; WHAT DOES THIS MEAN FOR THE BLACK RACE ON A WHOLE?

WE AS BLACK PEOPLE RAN OUT OF TIME YET AGAIN.

WE AS BLACK PEOPLE REJECTED THE TRUTH OF GOOD GOD AND ALLELUJAH; LOVEY, SO WHAT DOES THIS MEAN FOR US AS A RACE AND PEOPLE?

She (the black lady of Zion) lost her place. She failed to secure the black race, and I truly do not care if you look at it from a hue standpoint. I too am fed up of the bullshit of the black race and the shit we accept and say is ours when it is not. We sell ourselves short then turn around and blame everyone in the world for our misgivings a part from self. We as a race helped in creating this mess and we need to start fixing it by fixing self. We need to become self reliant and self sufficient instead of dependant on the crooked systems that surrounds us. Tupac told you this in CHANGES but yet we refuse to listen. Instead, we are stuck on the bullshit of slavery and repatriation. Bleep slavery and repatriation because a system of vultures and thieves cannot respect you nor can it and or they respect your values and God. All they can do is get you to accept their

<u>lies. Bob Marley told you this in AMBUSH IN THE NIGHT. He told us what we know is what they tell and or teach us. Listen to the song because this is our truth; knowledge.</u>

As a race we are being pitted against each other and we cannot see this because when some a wi get status they become sell outs. Sell outs in the sense that they buy into the lies of greed and self destruction; deprivation.

When some of us reach a certain level they tell you they are going to help you but help never comes. Dem a bag a mouth an bag a chat. All they do is keep you down and back. But that's okay because today a fi yu but tomorrow is so different. So I truly do not rely on my black own for anything, nor should anyone have to. As a race we are full of lies and hatred thus Michelle's Book Blog - Book 22. I am different thus I do not need an apology for what we the black race created. <u>We sold our people into slavery and until we accept the blame for our bullshit of lies when it comes to our true history; we will not be better as a people and nation.</u>

<u>Why want to be integrated and or assimilated in systems that are meant to keep us down; poor and weak?</u>

We are not a weak set of people. We are inventors, but yet to the shit we accept globally, you would and do think otherwise.

No shackles and chains could have come upon our feet and neck mentally and spiritually if we; our forefathers did not sell us out as a people.

<u>We accepted death. And by accepting death you must be punished. All must be taken from you and we have not figured this out yet.</u>

Di debil nuh like unnu!
Di debil caane stan unnu!

Why the hell do you think lands like Egypt, America, Jamaica and others were infiltrated? Many black lands hold and or held the keys to life; Lovey. <u>By us accepting the lies and participating in the lies of Babylon we condemned our self. And we did condemn our self. This is why Lovey is lost to us and we cannot find him. We have not learnt that Babylon is our enemy and from wi ha dem inna wi land good luck in finding and reaching Lovey. You must become the slaves of Babylon and this is what has and have happened to our ancestors and us until this day.</u>

Africa cannot be better until we give up the crap of Babylon including their language, customs, perverse bullshit of polygamy and more including their children and people; dress.

Why the bleep do you think they tell us if we accept Allah we become his servant.

<u>We are not Allah's servant, we are his children thus we have his breath of life. Meaning he's in us and he guides us.</u>

<u>Know this, when we join Islam we become these people's servants and we do not have a place with them apart from being their slaves.</u>

THEY DO NOT KNOW THE MEANING OF ALLAH.

THEY NEVER HAD ALLAH BECAUSE THEY HAVE NO LIFE. SUH DEM FOOL UNNU AN MEK UNNU CONDEMN UNNU SELF AND THIS IS WRONG ON THEIR PART. But we all knew that the devil was going to do all to take us from Lovey; Good God and Allelujah.

They had to get us to accept them and when we did that, accepted them; they destroyed our land, economy, praise (thanks), cleanliness and truth, customs, way of living and this is what has and have happened.

Thus Africa and African lands; all black lands are the way they are. Islam never belonged to them.

_Islam can never belong to them, thus THE TRUE ISLAM IS NO LONGER KNOWN TO US. WE ARE CUT OFF FROM IT THUS THE GARDEN OF EDEN ON ANOTHER LEVEL._

We did wrong and got kicked out AND _UNTIL THIS DAY WE CANNOT GET BACK IN._ Genesis

Like I said, the black woman of Zion lost. Now what then when it comes to the black race on a whole globally?

Look at the way I want to leave Lovey and he's been trying with me; securing my ass, but with all that said, I still want to leave him because of pain and loneliness; sorrow and hurt; financial and health woes; children woes and pain; suffering. I know we have to face the storm and I'm still facing the storm and he's not hearing me. Thus if father cannot hear; how can we as his children hear him and do that which is good and true; right for us and him?

If he keeps us broken, will we not be forever ever broken?

We are in hell and we keep telling him we want out and he keep us in hell, what are we left to do?

Are we not going to leave him?
Will we not complain and say he's not fair nor is he just?

How can he as a father say he wants us to live good and true; clean, but yet keep us in unclean surroundings and lands; environments?

Should he not do all in the spiritual and physical to protect his own if his own; good own is doing all to secure him by abiding by his law and laws; life?

He as Good God an Allelujah should know that there is so much our spirit and flesh can take. You don't keep us in prison and expect us to come out of prison if we do not have the key to open our prison walls; doors.

He Lovey should know that ABSOLUTELY NO ONE CAN KNOCK DOWN THE PRISON WALLS OF DEATH. COME ON NOW. Not even he Lovey can because HE LOVEY IS FORBIDDEN TO GO INTO HELL. HELL IS NOT CLEAN COME ON NOW.

Hell is where all unclean spirits are housed. Unclean spirits are sent there (to hell) to be punished; live out their sentence for the crimes and wrongs they've committed here on earth before their eventual death; extinction.

Hell is where demons reside come on now. Thus clean spirits cannot go there. We all know this.

So how is he Lovey expecting his children to go into hell and come out? Once we go into hell we become damaged goods.

WE EXPIRE BECAUSE THERE ARE NO RETURN TO SENDER WHEN IT COMES TO HELL. COME ON NOW.

ONCE YOU EXPIRE YOU EXPIRE.

THERE IS NO RETURN FOR YOU ONCE YOU GO TO HELL AND LOVEY KNOWS THIS. And if he doesn't know, now he knows.

He Lovey cannot say he's God and he's worthy to be praised and leave us confused, shamed and used; dead. Come on now.

If you are worthy to be praised, why leave us; abandon us so that we can't find you?

Don't tell me you are worthy to be praised; when the earth is in such disarray.

Don't tell me you are worthy to be praised; when humans globally kill the trees and waterways of life.

What about true and good life?

How is good life to feel when humans kill it daily?

*When you've done something constructive and true to good and true life tell me about praise.*

I'm sorry Lovey but I have to come hard to you in this way. Humans are not the only ones losing out when it comes to good and true life. Humans destroy good and true life, but yet you hang on to us for what?

*Why do you hang on to people that truly do not want you, people that constantly choose death over you?*

You are not wanted but yet it come eene like yu a beg wi fi accept an like yu.

Wi tell yu fi kiss wi ass an yu kiss it.

Coo pan di structure and disarray of earth. A people wey care bout yu destroy yu an yu creation like dis?

Death has all of humanity by the balls and there isn't a damned thing you can do about it. All you can do is look and walk away because we as humans made it this way.

*Yu nuh si sey yu dey pan di sidelines with rejected playing loud and clear for you to hear.*

Yu desperate?

Sin and Death laugh at you when it comes to humans and you still have not learnt.

Yes yu head bow down inna shame but WHOSE FAULT IS IT?

ARE YOU NOT TO BLAME FOR YOUR DISOBEDIENCE ALSO?

DID YOU NOT DISOBEY THE TRUTH OF THIS EARTH AND LIFE ITSELF?

WAS IT NOT THROUGH YOUR FOUNDATION THAT GOOD AND EVIL CAME?

DID YOU NOT GIVE ONE COLOUR MORE POWER OVER THE NEXT? So truly look at you because I am so not going to go easy on you. Yes I know I am wrong so truly forgive me, but you need to adhere to the truth and let us as humans and spirits go.

You have to let the evils in humanity go come on now.

Yes I know our spirit cannot survive without you, but if we as humans did not make you our good and true spiritual choice; then you have to truly go; let us go.

## You cannot save us.

## You have to leave us in goodness and in truth because we were the ones that did not choose goodness for self and spirit; You. Come on now.

Humans have proven to you time and time again that death is their choice.

Combined yearly, governments spend trillions of dollars on death whilst depriving humanity and or their people of their basic and rightful needs to life.

They condemn their land and people to hell. So tell me, where is the care and goodness when it comes to humans on a whole?

Look at how we as humans and spirit hate each other.

Look at how we as humans and spirit tell lies on each other.

We cannot live together in peace come on now.

So you cannot look to humans for goodness because we have no goodness in us come on now. If we did, the earth wouldn't be dying and we would not hate and kill each other each and every day.

If we truly cared and truly loved each other, we would not put enmity and strife between nations and kingdoms based on religious beliefs, sexual preference, hue and or skin tone, physical characteristics (fat and skinny), the way we speak and dress and so much more. We would not put enmity and strife between anyone or anything for that matter.

This is why I tell you to complete the separation and let evil and wicked people including lands and waterways, animals and spirit go more than infinitely and indefinitely without end more than forever ever.

## YOU CANNOT SAVE PEOPLE WHO CONSTANTLY TELL YOU THEY DON'T WANT YOU TO SAVE THEM.

## YOU CANNOT CONSTANTLY SEND MESSENGERS TO A RACE OF PEOPLE THAT WILL FOREVER EVER CONTINUE TO TELL YOU TO KISS THEIR ASS. THEY WOULD RATHER BE SLAVES AND LIVE IN MISERY RATHER THAN LIVE WITH YOU.

Look at me Lovey, HAVE I NOT TOLD YOU THIS?
Have I not told you I would rather take my chances with death than stay with you?

<u>So tell me, what do you not comprehend when it comes to the misery of our spirit and the turmoil that we face here on earth?</u>

There should not be a waiting game with you. If you see us truly trying, then truly help us and make our way easier come on now. And in doing this, helping us, make sure we stay with you in goodness and in truth.

Life is not about unfairness.

I've told you; if I could give you everything void of all sin and evil I would. I would give you all good, true and clean with more than my love of truth more than unconditionally. Come on now.

You are special to me but to me I am not truly special to you. You know my heartache and pain, woe and woes come on now. Do something to help me ease my pain and confusion when it comes to you; us and my surroundings including human family.

<u>The seeds you've given to me, I need to give them back to you good and true; pure, but you won't let me. So how can I be your saving grace if you can't even save me?</u>

You have my true love Lovey, so use it; my true love to heal you in a positive way. Never think I hate you because I truly don't. I need better for us and this earth come on now.

I NEED MOTHER AND FATHER TO JOIN IN TRUTH AND TRUE UNITY AND PROSPERITY.

You can't be against earth and earth be against you.

I'm in pain and earth is in pain. So let's get rid of the cancer and cancer sticks; people and spirits that plague us and this earth come on now.

You are my good and true choice and you cannot continue to ignore me and make me suffer. Tell me something; you want a mega mansion right?

So if you are not helping me positively and in a good way, how can I give you your good and true home; MEGA MANSION?

Truly think because you are truly not thinking when it comes to me in my view. Yes you can say otherwise, but this is my talk and my truth to you and you know this.

You are my mother and father, so why are you leaving me mother and fatherless?

Why do I feel abandoned?
Hopeless?

What about the trees and waterways of life Lovey, why abandon them and leave them for dead also?

What have they done to you for them to warrant your disrespect and disregard?

Humans destroy all that is good and true but yet you favour humans over the trees and waterways. So you are telling me, you are one sided and lopsided; you care not for truth. Hence ugly can tell me you answer them right away. Yes I am getting down on you because you are not fair to the waters and trees of life. I truly love them (the waterways and trees) but you truly don't.

WHY PUNISH THEM FOR THE WRONGS OF HUMANITY?

They did you no wrong or harm, but yet they are punished; killed.

Why let humans destroy it all?

Why do you see with humans and not see with the waterways and trees of life?

Do they not deserve your true love also? I chose you; good and true life and you have to include the waterways and trees of life. They are truly important to me; life.

Yes I am interrupting the flow of this book yet again but it cannot be helped. So don't get it twisted. <u>I truly love Lovey more than unconditionally, but there is too much evil here on this earth and we as black people truly do not listen.</u> We do not look into things and say, <u>we are the original inhabitants of this earth, why would he Lovey tell us to have dominion over the earth?</u>

Why would he tell us to subdue the earth if we are one with him; are a part of this earth?

<u>WHEN WE SUBDUE THE EARTH, ARE WE NOT DESTROYING IT; EARTH AND SELF?</u>

Are we not telling Lovey we want to control and dominate; kill the physical side of him; her?

Do we not beat the earth and kill all within earth?

So tell me Lovey, how can you stay sane in all of this?

If I am confused, are you not confused also?

So how can you truly love? You cannot because you can only love so.

Now tell me this Lovey, if I can love true and more than unconditionally; how come you can only love so?

Are we as father and daughter as well as mother and daughter not unbalanced?

Are we not unbalanced Lovey?

So how can we be true if we are not balanced; even in all of this; all that we do?

So what am I missing with you?
What are you missing with me?

We as black people fell from grace Lovey and instead of saying you know what, all the bullshit that I am forced to accept; I will no longer accept it; we do nothing constructive for self. We want you to do it all including me. Yes I know you cannot do all Lovey but this is me with you. I need you to think also. I need you to over stand and more than comprehend where I am coming from with my line of thinking and reasoning.

Yes I know many of us as blacks have and has become sell outs; the ones selling the bullshit and lies force fed to us so that we can intern feed the rest of black society the same bullshit if not worse.

<u>We constantly accept assimilation and or integration without KNOWING THAT SEGREGATION IS FUNDAMENTAL TO OUR EXISTANCE HERE ON EARTH.</u>

Why want to be integrated and assimilated in the devil's system of things; domain and or society?

Why do we constantly give up our truth; true life to become a part of a dead one; dead life?

Lovey, I truly do not know because as your chosen for these books, I truly want to walk away from my black own based on hue and nothing else.

I cannot comprehend them. Thus if the opportunity arise where I can give another race your truth I will. I am truly tired of black people rejecting you. So if you find it befitting to go to another race with this truth then let me go and truly lock the black race out. No Babylonians though. Trust me I am all for it as long as they (this race) do not reject you. Yes it would like the time of Moses all over again but without the stragglers (Babylonians).

You can't keep giving us as a people the truth and we keep turning from you then turn around and cry foul.

IF AFRICA IS NOT HELPING YOU WITH THE TRUE TRUTH; BLEEP AFRICA AND LET THEM STAND ON THEIR LYING AND DECEIVING OWN.

We can no longer support a race and or nation of vipers that know the truth but refuse to tell it. Instead they lie to humanity and sell out their black own.

Some go as far as call us slaves. Go figure Lovey. They are looked upon as slaves, but yet some have the nerve to call us slaves. If that isn't the pot calling the kettle black I truly don't know what is. Some need to take a look at the internet and see how they are depicted.

TELL ME SOMETHING LOVEY. HOW THE HELL CAN YOU BE THE FIRST BUT YET KNOW NOT YOUR TRUE ROOTS; HISTORY. THAT TELLS ME YOU WERE NEVER THE FIRST. YOU'RE ALL FRAUDS BECAUSE NOTHING TRUTHFUL COMES OUT OF MOTHER AFRICA UNTIL THIS DAY.

Go ahead and say it and let me school you because YOU CANNOT BE and or say YOU ARE THE FIRST AND KNOW NOT CREATION COME ON NOW.

YOU CANNOT BE THE FIRST AND KNOW NOT HOW LIFE; ALL LIFE CAME INTO BEING.

YOU CANNOT BE THE FIRST AND KNOW NOT THE TRUTH OF YOUR HERITAGE; HISTORY AND DOMAIN COME ON NOW.

YOU CANNOT SAY YOU ARE THE FIRST AND KNOW NOT THE EARTH AND THE SPIRITUAL REALM INCLUDING LOVEY HIMSELF. We have the breath of life in us, but yet as black people; the first creation we know this not.

SO AS THE WORLD HAVE AND HAS DECEIVED, SO AS AFRICA; THE CHILDREN AND PEOPLE OF AFRICA DECEIVED THE WORLD ALSO.

COME ON NOW KNOW THE TRUTH.

GREATNESS WAS NEVER IN YOU IF YOU CAN'T TELL THE TRUTH COME ON NOW. You say you are but you are truly not. In truth, I saw the first creation but was not shown what land he came out of. I know where life started, but no one can say human life; the origins of humanity started in Africa. Yes Africa is the hub, womb and center of life, but what life?

Africa is the center of life but it is also the center and hub of death. Thus life and death came out of Africa and until this day we cannot figure this out.

NO BLACK MAN CAN TALK ABOUT AFRICA WITHOUT INCLUDING ASIAN LAND BECAUSE THESE TWO LANDS ARE THE SAME.

Thus you cannot talk about life without talking about the Ying and Yang; Asia. THUS DUE TO INTEGRATION AND OR ASSIMILATION AND OR COLONIZATIONS BLACKS GLOBALLY HAVE NO TRUE ROOTS; KNOW NOT THE TRUTH.

WE LOST OUR TREE OF LIFE AND THAT TREE OF LIFE IS LOVEY. NO MATTER HOW WE TRY TO FIND HIM WE CANNOT. HE DID LEAVE US BECAUSE WE KEEP SELLING HIM OUT BY ACCEPTING LIES AND FALSE DOCTRINES THAT TELL LIES ON HIM.

Yes Lovey I know your true love of me but I need more from you and yes you can call me greedy for this.

Yes I've chosen you but what good is choosing you when we as a people are lost; confused?

Thus I dedicate IT WOULD BE YOU by Johnny Gill to you because you are my everything and IT IS YOU. I've chosen you as my good and true friend and partner in life. Thus come December 2015 let the confusion stop all around. Let the black race begin to listen and walk away from all that is wicked and evil; sinful.

<u>We can no longer leave you stuck on the sideline waving your flag and yelling choose me if you want life and a better way of life.</u>

We can no longer ignore you because you are our saving grace come on now.

Listen Lovey, I am expecting all that is good and true from you. YOU ARE MORE THAN MY BODY GUARD, SO GUARD ME TRUE. I know the backlash that is coming. It matters not to me as long as I truly have you in all that I do. I need you to know this. Tell me something Lovey, how will I survive without you?

How can I go on without you?

So as of December 2015 let each and every day be our day and days of truth and goodness. I don't want to lose you, but I truly do not need the confusion and heartache. Nor do I need the I am leaving you in my life anymore.

Truly listen to IT WOULD BE YOU because I did choose and chose you. So truly think. Someone did truly love you but you are the neglectful one in all of this.

I cannot speak for all of humanity; I can only speak on the behalf of myself. You are needed in my life. You are my true life line.

I've told you, if I could give you this world honest and true, pure and clean; whole, I would.

If I could create a world and universe void of all hate and sin; shame and uncleanliness, I would just for me and you and our good and true children and people.

No other god will do when it comes to me hence I cling to you, bug you, cuss you, rest my head on your shoulders, laugh and cry with you and for you. My heart of truth belongs to you. It is crying out to you for you to see and notice me; read the lines of truth in some of these books. I need you to be okay with me and what I do for you in goodness and truth. So take this song IT WOULD BE YOU by Johnny Gill and feel my emotions in song and words for you.

I need to abide with you but I cannot abide with you in a land I truly don't want to be in. Please listen to me Lovey and truly complete me; make me whole in self; spirit and in you.

You are my director, so direct me in goodness and in truth. All the goodness I have for you must share for us, me and you, my gorgeous mother and our people; our good and true family. So tell me why is this not enough for you; us?

Is my true love for you tainted Lovey?

Why isn't my truth enough for you?

Why isn't my true love good enough to save our good and true people; me and you?

Life is worth it but sometimes with you, I get the feeling that life isn't worth it.

So tell me, what is the point of saying you love so when you cannot protect me more than infinitely and indefinitely from all evil. You see me but it's as if you truly do not know me. You care about evil and wicked people; ugly people more than me.

What is the point of saying you love so when your people; our good and people are being led astray?

What is the point of saying you love so when your people; our good and true people are being kept from you?

Am I missing something with you and life Lovey?

Tell me, what is life without you?

What purpose do we serve when it comes to you Lovey if we are in doubt of you; can't find you?

I know our ancestors let you go and when we let you go; no matter how much we search we cannot find you. But is this what you want for us Lovey?

Do you want me to become a wonderer and vagabond without you?

You are my choice but why am I not good enough for you? Why do I feel neglected, used and abused by you?

All I know is; I need you. Many of us here on earth need you but you are not truly there.

<u>Yes I know the unclean environments we live in and the death we accept. But Lovey, at the end of the day, we are looking to you for guidance. We need you to guide our way so that we can walk upright and true out of Babylon and come back to you.</u>

So tell me now Lovey. What good is making you Lovey our infinite and indefinite good and true foundations and frameworks, when you cannot protect our foundations and frameworks all around?

This is not just for me but our good and true people. We need to be free to walk, but we are not free to walk and roam this earth because the majority of places on earth are corrupt; filled with evil.

Lovey I know as humans we took our truth and true love from you, but what about the ones who've found their way home back to you?

What does our truth mean to you?
What does our life mean to you?

You are getting truth from me Lovey, so why stay away from me?

Why leave me at the wayside and or the roadside for dead?

I don't know because I cannot write to you like this anymore. No life can exist without you and you know this, but yet you cannot see this; you don't want to see this. And in truth, I truly do not blame you. We did do you wrong all around. You did try with us, we were the ones to neglect and reject you.

You are the foundation of life and as the foundation of life you have to be true to all.

_As humans we have choices but what good is our choice if our choice is not good and true life; truth?_

No other god or gods can replace Lovey and we all know this but yet we choose other gods over him. We bow down to false idols and gods instead of living our life good and true; clean.

We all know and see the issues and problems facing us here on earth, but instead of fixing these issues and problems; governments spend money to escalate them. We spend more on death without seeing the value of life; self and people.

We as humans also contribute to this because we continue to have children that we cannot afford; thus over populating this earth.

We keep electing people into political office that have not our best interest at heart. Men and women that value not and or respect the sanctity and sanctuary of life.

MEN AND WOMEN WHO SEEK TO CONTROL; KILL.

MEN AND WOMEN WHO TAKE AWAY OUR RIGHT AND RIGHTS TO FREEDOM; THE BASIC NECESSITY OF LIFE.

MEN AND WOMEN WHO RULE WITH A IRON FIST.

MEN AND WOMEN WHO LEAVE THEIR OWN PEOPLE; CITIZENS HOMELESS AND PENNILESS WHILE THEY SPEND HUNDREDS OF MILLIONS AND BILLIONS EACH YEAR ON WAR; DEATH; WAR MACHINES.

<u>So as humans we need to set priorities for our self. We as humans need to govern our life and not let others govern it for us.</u>

Many of us do not sit and look into things. We do not value our life and spirit; self.

<u>We let others condition our way of life and thought and this is truly wrong. You are the controller of your spirit and life, so control and or secure your life; spirit.</u>

No one knows you but you and you have to do right and good; true for you and by you. <u>Truly look at the world today and see what the politicians of this world have and has done to earth and your life. You are caught up in their mess and earth is caught up in it too.</u>

What gives a man or woman including child the right to take away from our lives because of greed, hate; dominance and control?

<u>What good is leading your citizens if you are going to control them; exterminate them by any means necessary?</u>

Thus the tyranny of demented and mentally unstable men and women of the past and today. Men and women including children that feel they have the right to do whatever they want to do to you because they have power and control.

Men and some women who feel that ALL THE EVILS THEY DO ON EARTH THEY CAN AND WILL GET AWAY WITH IT.

<u>Men and woman who knows not the spirit and the dangers; brutally of the spiritual world that is going to be inflicted on them due to the judgment of their own sin and sins.</u>

Yes Lovey is my best friend and I truly do not want to hurt him, but he need to stop hurting me; us. Truth does not hurt; thus he's not truthful to me and this I am finding out.

Maybe it's me and he cannot give me what I want. He see the future and knows the future. But with all this said; I am truly not happy. I need to find my happiness without him and yes to a large extent with him.

I need nature. I crave and trust nature with every fabric of my being and truth. I am not happy nor am I content without nature. It's like if I could rip the earth apart and walk to nature I would. This is how my spirit is going crazy. _Thus the spirit can go mad; insane._

We want him Lovey to do while we continue doing wrong and this cannot happen. We made the mess in our lives and we are the ones that must fix them.

We have to sit down with the ones we err including self and come up with a viable solution in regards cleaning up our mess.

Without a plan; a good and true; honest and clean plan we cannot succeed and this is what I am finding out. Yes for some of us our plans do not work out. But that plan was not the right plan.

Did that plan have all the elements you needed?
Was that plan true to you and your surroundings?
Was that plan true to life; God and or Lovey?

Yes we all can come up with great plans, but what good is that plan if it does not include your surroundings; all?

It's like my son; last child made a career choice. He told me what he wants to do in life. I am encouraging him but you know what?

I can encourage all I want but if he does not have a plan; a good and true, honest and clean plan, he will never achieve his destiny.

You cannot say you want to be a doctor (he doesn't want to be a doctor), but you cannot say you want to be a doctor and don't research what courses you need to take in high school in order to help you achieve your goal and or aim.

_You have to take life serious because your high school years are critical to your future. If you are not future ready by the time you reach high school then you are lost. You will fail in some areas and the time wasted in high school is time wasted when it comes to your future._

Well some men; rich men and woman did not go to university or college.

Great for them, but have you thought about what some did to get where they are at? THUS WHAT DOES IT PROFIT YOU TO GAIN IT ALL AND TO LOSE YOUR

SOUL AND OR SPIRIT IN THE END? The rich man hath no soul and or spirit if they live for greed and deceit; destruction. I've seen the spirit of the rich and it's not pretty. You can have riches but you have to live clean and honest, and some truly don't. So they too (the rich) must take heed and try to correct their unclean and or dirty ways if they want to be saved.

Life isn't flesh, **_it's spirit_** and I've told you this. What you can get away with in the physical you cannot and will not get away with it in the spiritual realm.

## The spiritual realm is your TRUE COURT HOUSE; HOUSE OF LAW AND JUSTICE.

THUS THE LIFE YOU LIVE IN THE LIVING DETERMINES WHERE YOU GO UPON DEATH; THE SPIRIT SHEDDING THE FLESH FOR WHICH SOME OF US CALL DEATH.

### THE SPIRIT IS WHAT GIVES THE FLESH LIFE.

### ONCE THE SPIRIT IS GONE, THE FLESH GOES BACK TO ITS ORIGINAL SOURCE. So truly know you because if you cannot take the heat of earth, you cannot and will not be able to take the heat of hell. This heat; the heat of hell is infinitely hotter than that of our sun because we are the ones to create hell with our sins.

The spirit can go though the fire of the sun and live but the spirit cannot survive nor can it go through the fire and or fires of hell. The fire and or fires of hell was specifically designed and or created for the spirit by you. Your sins and to a certain extent, the sins of others and our forefathers determine your stay in this fire.

So if you have not petitioned Lovey for their sins truly good luck. And yes if you are good and clean and you truly love, you can petition Lovey for the ones that you truly love. Just as how I petition him for my mother, my children and the good and true seeds he's given me, as well as certain family members you can too. **_NEVER FORGET THAT A JEW; TRUE JEW IS NOT GOVERNED BY THE LAWS OF MAN AND OR MEN; THEY ARE GOVERNED BY THE LAWS OF GOD; LOVEY; FOR WHOM I CALL GOOD GOD AND ALLELUJAH._**

Right now, the debts of humanity cannot be repaid; it keeps growing and this is why destruction comes also.

Humanity keep forgetting that the longer we put off paying for our debts the longer we stay in hell. It's like this, when a Prime Minister and or President rack up the national debt of your country, the debt grows (collects interest). When he or she leaves office someone else takes on that debt and adds more debt to that debt. So the debt keeps growing and growing and this is what's happened to a lot of countries. The debt gets so bad and high that some countries cannot pay their debt and some lands do go bankrupt. But what you do not comprehend is, it matters not if the land and or your land go bankrupt when it comes to death. You still owe him and he's going to get paid no matter what. He will take you the citizen of the land because all death has to do is point at your land's unpaid debt. This is the same scenario in our lives expect our bankruptcy is death; death taking your spirit at will and bringing it to hell with him.

Thus truly know your sins. Yes I know for billions of you it's hard to pay your debt physically and financially. I'm in that bracket too but with the physical debt. For some of us; **_our parents don't tell us some men and women that we pick up blight wi life indefinitely._** *Trust me I learnt the hard way that some man you just don't pick up and procreate with because they are true demons. They have no soul; hence they prey off you and feed off you physically and spiritually.*

Some of you like to pray for people in the name of God without knowing the person and this sinful practice has to stop. That person could be a mass murderer and you are praying for him or her. When you do this, you take on that person's sins because you are seeking favour for wrongs; the wrongs he or she committed and or did.

**Before you even pray for someone, ask Lovey for permission first. Some sins are truly not forgiven, so how can you or I go to Lovey and petition him for forgiveness for the next man or woman; person's sin and sins WHEN WE TRULY DO NOT KNOW THEM?**

If you want a good and true person in your life, pray to Lovey for that good and true person.

## <u>Yes we all fall down but you cannot stay down; you have to get back up. It may take you longer than others but you have to try even when you don't want to.</u>

Sometimes Lovey have to knock us down for us to see.

He knocks you down and let you be tested brutal and hard this I know.

Wow Allelujah because I've faced the storm and storms in my life and still facing them.

It isn't easy. You are rocked and tossed like a rag doll sometimes but you cannot give up.

All when you give up pick yourself up and move on.

Disrespect does come from your children, their friends and your family. But you have to get past this disrespect. You will overcome this.

People will look down on you and you have to get past this too. Like I said above, today a fi dem but tomorrow is for you. Tomorrow could be three months from now, a year or ten years from now. But know; tomorrow is for you and it does come.

## RIGHT NOW; TODAY AFFI DI DEBIL, BUT TOMORROW AFFI LOVEY.

It's taken Lovey 24000 for truth to fully come to earth and shortly this truth will fully reign. The time is set in the future and or in time and it's a matter of when we get there if you can comprehend what I am saying.

### Lovey has patiently waited for this truth to come and it's here. It's up to you to see this and amend your dirty ways. HE CANNOT SAVE YOU IF YOU ARE DIRTY COME ON NOW.

No. Trust me forces come in your way for you to fail. People talk crap for you to fail so truly know them.

You are tried and tested by your family, children, friends and spirits.

Sometimes your health take a toll on you.
You become lonely and depressed.

You have heartache and pain, but you cannot give up because you have to go through trials and tribulations.

**_It was not always like this, but know that evil; wicked and evil spirits and people want and need you to fail. One victory for Lovey is time lost for death._**

One soul and or spirit lost to Lovey for evil drives death crazy; no not death but Satan. Satan does not like to lose; thus his people do all to get you to sin; sell your soul and or spirit to death and or him Satan.

**_We've all sinned I know, but you have help; you. Like I've told you over and over again in some of my other books; a dirty person cannot pray for you and you become clean. You will remain dirty and become dirtier. So truly know who prays for you because that dirty person's sin and sins are added unto you. So if you had one_**

_sin and that person has 50 million sins; his and or her 50 million sins become yours also. And I've told you this in another book._

As humans we cannot continue to allow dirty people to pray for us and tell us crap. They are in hell already; so why want to go to hell with them?

Why want to join them? Come on now

_Life isn't about death and if you don't know life you cannot live life, nor can you see Life; Lovey._

It's September 25, 2015 and I've been dreaming about rape, me being raped. I know I am stepping out in a avenue; new avenue for my books, but I cannot be scared. I also cannot let myself be careless. Family, my true family, I truly don't know when it comes to me at this stage, but like I said, I cannot be fearful, nor can I live my life in fear. I have to do for me and make a way for me. I cannot sit down and say goods things are going to happen to me and for me when I know they are not. I have to put forth an effort in opening doors for myself. Thus I have to get off my ass and do and not be so anti social.

I need something and I have to seek it. Yes I've been trying for years and no solid doors are opening for me, but I can't give up. I have to keep on trying because I know where I want and need to be. I have to prepare a good and safe, true and positive future and environment for me and you. So I have to press on and move on.

Listen family, my true family. In life, if you want good and true for yourself you have to face your fears, and you must go on the battlefield. No, not fight war by killing, but you have to struggle. Struggles are going to come your way and you have to be strong in order to overcome. I know my struggles in life and sometimes I want to give up, and do give up on that day. But when tomorrow; the next day come, I am good to go and I press onwards again.

Wow, trust me you have to be strong especially if you have children. I don't know because it seems that the children of today, well some of mine have no self worth or value for themselves.

Trust me; if I make it financially, some of my children are going to cry. All that I get is going to go towards children that want and need a proper education and can't get it. _**IT MAKES NO SENSE TO SACRIFICE YOUR WELL BEING AS A PARENT AND YOUR CHILDREN HAVE NO AMBITION FOR SELF TO MOVE FORWARD EDUCATIONALLY.**_ Give to those that need; not to those that do not need. Come on now. I can't be showing you the way and you are telling me you don't want. I can't do it all, so truly help me come on now.

You push and push and all you ask for as a parent is to go to school and they don't want to go. They mess up and then when they mess up they cry foul. If you do not go to class regularly, if you do not study, if you walk the hallways of your school, if you are the class clown, how do you expect to get ahead?

Are you not wasting your time, the teacher's time and your classmate's time?

All the things you are not to do; you do, hence setting yourself up for failure and you do fail. You are behind thus you are jeopardizing your future. You want to do this as your future career, but if you do not buckle down and do all you can to be future ready how are you going to achieve; be future ready?

Don't say you've changed when you have not changed. Be true to you, and do all you can to build you in a positive way.

Thus I am finding that this, this future generation have no ambition for self. They want everything to be handed to them without working for it and it cannot be. As parents we can talk all we want, but some of these kids truly do not listen including mine. So you have to make them crash and burn and this is so what I am going to do to mine. I am giving them the easy way but they've proven to me that they want things the hard way except for one. So what I can do for the one that takes good counsel, I will do. It is only fair and just; right.

If you want better for self change your dirty ways and get off your ass and do something positive for you. Ole people sey, sidung neva sey git up yet and they are so true. Your ass can't tell you to get up; only your mind can, so get up and do in truth for you. Let your goodness radiate through you and when you do this, you are giving back to your environment. You may not see it but you are. Stop attracting negative forces and stop giving them (negative forces) your energy. Yes you will get angry at times, but calm yourself by reading your favorite book, listen to soothing music or just take some quiet alone time for you to think. Come on now.

Yes it's October 01, 2015 and I truly don't know what is happening anymore in the spirit world. I keep dreaming about this calm; calm waters.

Florida, I truly don't know about you because I can't remember if your land was devastated again.

Dreamt I was in a church. The lady was a black female. I cannot tell you if this church is a Zionist church. All I can tell you is that I took this rope; black rope that the leader of this church spoke with in her mouth. This black rope was in her mouth while speaking for those of you who want to know. I was talking and or preaching and when I was finished she came and I took the rope out of my mouth; washed the black rope (noose like rope) and gave it back to her. I can't remember if I put it back in her mouth, but I know I washed it and gave it back to her. Upon doing that a elder of a Zionist church I used to go to (yes I use to go to church) came in. I don't know what I was doing but I think someone was talking about me and he elder said my full name; (first and last name) and I answered him. He had money in his pocket and he took out a wad and or roll of money and broke it in half. He gave me half and some other people some of the money but I got half. He said; this money is for someone else. Strange but I am so going to leave things alone. I have no idea what the money represent. The black noose I was using to talk and gave back to her, this black woman, I am hoping I was giving death back to her. _**I am hoping my life and words will not be about death anymore but about good and true life.**_

Family and people, I see so much death that I need to show and tell you just how beautiful life is going to be for Lovey's chosen few.

Dreamt about my brother but I have to leave this dream alone because I truly cannot remember it.

Dreamt some other things that I think have to do with children and or the younger generation but I cannot remember the dream. Thus black youths it's time for you to shape up because in all that you think you know, you truly do not know. Many of you are sitting and waiting on inheritance money that may never come. Rise up and have some ambition. Do not depend on mommy and daddy for all. If you can help yourself from now, help yourself in a good and true; positive way.

The end of man not time is here. If you are not living right, you will not survive the harvest that is coming. Like I said, the waters of life is calm and I truly don't know why. I truly don't know if this is the calm before the storm.

I know you've all heard this before but so far, many of what I've dreamt and told you about in these books have come to pass. **_I do not stay on course as to timeline because timelines are not for me to figure out. You all can given the dates I see these dreams to the time they happen. It's time to prepare because the Exodus is now._**

We have to begin to leave if we want to be saved come on now. I am just waiting for Lovey to tell me to gather his people. So truly do not get left behind in all of this. Yes you can doubt me, but what do I have to gain in all of this?

Think.

If I take your soul, how can you save me?
If I teach you wrong, how can you save me?

Will you not have me and mark me for death with death?

Life is given and I am telling you to live. ***A dead man hath no life anywhere.*** So do not continue to live and speak as the dead come on now.

EVIL CANNOT BE SAVED BECAUSE NO ONE IS ORDAINED TO SAVE THE WICKED AND EVIL; SINFUL COME ON NOW.

NO ONE CAN SAVE A WICKED AND EVIL PERSON. DEATH WILL NOT ALLOW THIS NOR WOULD LOVEY. THE WICKED AND EVIL ARE NOT HIS PEOPLE; THEY ARE DEATH'S TRUE PEOPLE.

Michelle and Michelle Jean

Oh Lovey what am I missing in the Southern Hemisphere as I call it and or below the Tropic of Capricorn?

My head is starting to hurt Lovey because I truly cannot figure it out.

I am missing something, but what I truly do not know.

Answer me this Lovey. Is all of Oceania going to sink eventually?

Is the Pacific Plate collapsing a micro scale?

Who knows, but I am so missing something in the South Pacific region literally.

Michelle
October 01, 2015

It's October 09, 2015 and there is more that I want to add to this book but I won't. I will leave those writings and create another book called MY THOUGHTS/FREEDOM. Yes the book will be short and spicy; no, not spicy but insightful I hope.

Yesterday I finished editing this book and went on Twitter and I retweeted some tweets. I especially retweeted Danny Glover's visit to Jamaica and the message he brought. I also retweeted the tweets about this man that committed suicide due to the scamming that's going on in Jamaica; thus MICHELLE'S BOOK BLOG - BOOK 23 JAMAICAN SCAMMER.

Fam and people; my true family, I went off brutal in this book so bad and furious that I cannot upload this book and will not upload this book to the furiousness and content of this book.

I know I've talked about scamming and or the scamming that is going on in the land, but it's beyond me.....no, let's leave that alone because no one can tell me about **_BLACKNESS AND BLACK POWER._** Anyone come to me with their black power; how black people are struggling mentally and spiritually and how we are shackled and chain made slaves, **_I GIVE YOU MY WORD THAT I WILL CUSS THEM FEROCIOUS AND BRUTAL._** No one can tell me about shackles and chains. None better come to me with their slavery bullshit either because like I've said time and time again; humans made other humans into slaves and blacks did sell their own people into slavery. Thus human trafficking is still predominant and or still global until this day.

I will not buy into your slavery bullshit because right there in Jamaica people are trafficked; sold to people in the United States of America and absolutely nothing is being done about it. So truly bleep the black race because we do shit and crap and expect others to pay for it.

Am I disappointed in my Jamaican own?

Yes I am. No one should rape another human being of what they've worked so damned hard for. The elderly wuk fi dem pay so that when they get older they can retire with a better life. But it's not all that can retire and enjoy their life because what they put down is not enough to life on.

Many put a little something away for their grandchildren and children.

Some can't afford to do so, so they play the lottery in hopes of winning so that their children and grandchildren can have a better life and future.

So why the hell should someone come in and scam them of their future; rob them of their net worth come on now?

Listen I do not care about the content or character of that person because I know what it's like to be robbed of everything in the spiritual and physical world.

I know the anguish and pain; thus I talk to Lovey in a certain way. You've built your life so that your future will not be harsh, but yet someone robs you of your life and future. Do you know how hard that person has to work to achieve and attain that future?

You've put nothing in that person's future but yet you rob them of all. Who the bleep are you to do this?

*You did not work for it, I did, so why should and or you taking it from me?*

*What did the elderly do to Jamaicans for Jamaicans to be robbing them of their finances and life?*

Yes unemployment is high on the island, but some a di young people dem don't want to work. Yu tell dem pick up farming dem tell yu dem han too clean. If you do not work for something, how are you going to get anything?

The government can only support you for so long and in some cases, the government do not support you.

Some a unnu sit a roadside waiting fi rob people. Some a unnu nuh value life.

Some, yu tell dem eat a food, and dem accept di money an kill yu; eat a food because the dead is their food.

Some just don't bleeping care as long as dem see duppy. Dem walk and live fi kill.

Some politicians extort business owners and if they are not paid their blood and or extortion money that business owner is killed.

Some live a obeah man an oman.

Some join lodge and or secret societies where they have to perform sacrifices; human and animal sacrifices in order to live. They kill you and get away with it. Thus the murders, rapes and sins that goes on in these societies stay in these societies; thus the secrecy of them. **_But there are no secrets in secret societies because DEATH KEEPS THE SECRECT FOR NO ONE._**

All this we do in Jamaica without knowing that all that we do; plunge land and people further into hell.

_When I see and read this, (scamming); what do we as a race and nation leave people to think about us?_

_Are we not giving people globally reasons not to trust Jamaicans and black people on a whole?_

_Are we not the ones to sink the black race and communities globally into hell?_

We talk about black pride, but we have no black pride to the crap government and people let happen in black lands.

So bleep black pride. When black people on a whole globally have self worth and self value then they can talk to me. And I don't give a rats ass how rich you are, you have no self worth because some of **_YOU RICH BLACK FOLKS, DEATH OWNS THE LOTS OF YOU._**

MANY OF YOU SIGNED A CONTRACT WITH DEATH FOR MONEY AND FAME. THUS THE LODGE SOCIETIES MANY OF YOU BELONG TO.

YOU'VE ALL KILLED YOUR FRIENDS AND FAMILY INCLUDING STRANGERS TO BE ACCEPTED IN THE DEVIL'S SOCIETY; THUS SHE THANKED ME FOR OUTING YOU ONE BY ONE.

We talk the talk, but yet we are the same ones selling each other and bringing our race and people to shame with the actions we do. Thus black people are not valued globally. We have not self worth and we cannot see this. Like I've said in other books, **_HELL IS FULL OF BLACK PEOPLE AND RECRUITING MORE._**

Satan can put im pot pan fiya and within a nana second or less we sell out self and others including Lovey for a place with him Satan.

WHY THE HELL DO YOU THINK SATAN LOVE BLACK PEOPLE SO MUCH? WE ARE NOT LOYAL TO ANYONE OR ANYTHING, BUT YET WE HAVE THE NERVE TO CRY TO LOVEY FOR HELP AFTA WI DONE SELL HIM OUT.

Yes I cussed out Death brutal yesterday because it seems all death can do is taunt me about the destruction of Jamaica. A mi alone death ha mouth fa it seems.

Listen, it matters not if these called centers are owned by multinationals and or if the leader of this operation reside out of the country; Jamaica. The fact is, the calls are coming out of your land and it is Jamaica and Jamaicans on a whole the world is looking at. We are the ones letting the world see us in a negative light because of our negative actions and or behaviour. It matters not about me and my cussing in these books because no one can stand to me and tell me to accept their bullshit. You want to bully me, well bully this because I know one day Lovey will hear me when I cry and you will be punished severely.

NO JAMAICAN ON THE FACE OF THIS PLANET CAN SAY SOMEONE ELSE CAUSED JAMAICA TO BE DESTROYED. JAMAICANS ARE THE ONES TO CAUSE JAMAICA TO BE DESTROYED. WE ALONE DID THIS TO SELF BECAUSE WE KEEP ACCEPTING THE OFFERINGS OF THE DEVIL AND HIS PEOPLE WITHOUT KNOWING WHEN WE DO THIS; LOVEY TURNS FROM US INDEFINITELY AND THIS IS WHAT'S HAPPENED TO JAMAICA.

WE'VE PROVEN TO HIM LOVEY TIME AND TIME AGAIN THAT WE AS A PEOPLE; RACE OF PEOPLE AND NATION THAT HE CANNOT TRUST US.

WE KEEP CRYING WOLF AND HE KEEPS BAILING US OUT ONLY FOR US TO GO RIGHT BACK INTO THE MESS AND MESSES HE'S TAKEN US OUT OF.

# HE'S GIVEN US MESSENGERS AND WE DENIED THEM.

_So no I do not feel mercy for my own because my own truly do not have mercy for self and others. Instead of building we continue to break down and ruin. We are the ones that are ruining the reputation of the black race globally._

We are the ones killing self and I will not blame another nation for this. We know of our own misgivings and instead of correcting them we continue on with them.

So no, stay in hell because Black People truly do not want and need better for self. It's time to stop writing and singing and do for self. _You know there's good life at the end of the rainbow. Stop sitting down on your ass and expect the gold to walk to you. You have to walk to it in order to get it. If you don't someone else is going to see it and walk to it; take it._ and this is what has happened to you Jamaica and black people on a whole.

_Lovey's home should have been built in you (Jamaica) but because of wickedness and sins; filth, Lovey deemed Jamaica unclean._ And no, you don't have to take my word for it, ASK HIM LOVEY because the sign and or writing in the Blue and White sky read JamaicaF and I've told you this. This is how I saw it and this is how I am relating it back to you.

**Like I said, he gave us all of him and we are the ones to ruin him and destroy all that he's given us. Thus many of you, if not all of you are going to pay shortly.**

As for Michelle's Book Blog – Book 23 Jamaican Scammer there are just some of the things I said in book.

I will leave out the wicked and evil stuff. And do forgive me for the swearing but it cannot be helped. And yes I did swear reckless and rude in the book. Once again, I am truly sorry for the swearing because I had no intent or intentions of putting swearing in this book. My book blogs are that serious and harsh; thus they are not holds barred. Thus I gave you the minimal swearing parts. So as I close this book, truly enjoy.

Michelle

# Except from Michelle's Book Blog – Book 23 Jamaican Scammer

Lovey I am tired hence these people that Jamaicans are scamming must be vindicated and right away.

I will not petition death anymore for the land of Jamaica. I have to let Jamaica go because I cannot fathom life when it comes to them.

You gave these ignorant so and so your name and breath of life and we destroyed you and self like this!

So tell me, how can anyone in the world trust a Jamaican including me and you considering what Jamaicans are doing to the elderly?

Wow Lovey because I am truly sorry. Sorry that you chose me to be born in that land on this day to what I see and what's going on in that land.

I know it's possible, but I regret you choosing me to represent you in writing due to what's happening in Jamaica and what they are doing.

YES I KNOW IT'S NOT ALL THAT IS DOING IT, BUT IT MIGHT AS WELL BE TO THE WAY I FEEL RIGHT NOW.

MI FEEL SHAME AND HOLD MY HEAD AND SPIRIT DOWN IN SHAME AND DISGRACE.

I know I should not be saying this, but I have to tell you the way I feel. Lovey I cherish and adore you so much and to read what Jamaicans are doing to seniors; the elderly brings tears to my eyes.

So now tell me, why you chose Jamaica when you knew they would dishonour and disgrace you like this?

Why give them your name and breath of life when you knew they would turn against you and do all that is wicked and evil in thy sight?

Why Lovey, truly why?

Why continue to try with us when we do all that is wicked and evil in the land; home you've given us?

You trusted us and we kill you all around.

We caused you to flee from that land; hence YOU DID DEEM IT UNCLEAN.

So why should I petition you or death for any of them?

Let them fucking rot and burn in hell because none deserve you period.

We're a bunch of sell outs and turn coats that value nothing but the sins and deplorable acts they commit; do.

Trust me, they are my own but I am beginning to loathe them and the land that they live and or reside in.

I don't care if they hate me but fair is fair come on now.

None would like anyone to scam them and take their livelihood from them, but yet they do it to another human being.

And to top it off, those disgusting and shameful scum buckets that reside in the house of parliament isn't doing anything constructive to catch these scammers. Thus it would not surprise me if the majority of them is involved.

They are all a bunch of fucking jokes that cannot see that the scamming bullshit that is happening there is hurting the reputation of Jamaica.

NO WONDER SOME JAMAICANS REFUSE TO COME BACK THERE LITERALLY.

No come on Lovey. I was bugging you to go back there and say mi a guh bi disobedient an guh dey. Figet eee. I refuse to go back there; thus I am truly happy and proud you chose another island to build and or have your good and true home in.

I truly don't need my Jamaican own because we have no conduct or content of character to be doing this bullshit.

No Lovey, don't taunt me because the evil and evils of that land is more than astounding for you to deem Jamaica unclean due to its wicked and sell out people dem.

Yes I know death will not like my words but frankly Lovey, I truly don't give a damn. When death grow some balls he and she can come talk to me thus they have none.

How can anyone find beauty anymore in this filthy cesspool of a land?

Yes I went there and all a unnu inna Jamaica can cuss mi, but cuss mi fi di truth.

Unnu nuh tun Jamaica into the DUNG OF HELL WITH THE BULLSHIT THAT IS HAPPENING DAILY ON THE LAND?

Look into unnu self and tell me if the scamming and bullshit you do daily on the island is worth it?

Unnu lose unnu place with Lovey; God because unnu dutty.

So tell me, who the hell is going to save the lots of you because mi tun mi back pan unnu literally. Don't even chat to mi back.

Kip unnu dutty and stinking island because it is NOW BEFITTING FOR LOVEY TO TAKE AWAY FROM THE LIFE OF ANYONE THAT GOES THERE TO VACATION.

AND BECAUSE UNNU CAUSE A HUMAN BEING TO TAKE HIS LIFE DUE TO JAMAICAN SCAMMING, LOVEY MUST TAKE AWAY FROM THE LIFE OF EVERY JAMAICAN GLOBALLY. Yes this includes me because I was born in that land. But I petition him Lovey for my life and for the life of the good people that still reside there and globally; that he may not take away from our life.

So Lovey, truly hear my plea and protect me, my children and family including the good and true seeds you have give me, the good and true Jamaicans globally and leave our life intact in and with you in goodness and in truth more than forevermore.

TRULY LET THE EVILS THAT THESE SCAMMERS DO, TURN BACK ON THEM; BEFALL THEM BECAUSE THEY DID TAKE A LIFE AND THEY ARE TAKING AWAY LIFE FROM ALL THE GOOD AND TRUE JAMAICANS GLOBALLY. Thus if it be thy will, give me back a good and true; truly clean and whole; positive Jamaica for me and you and our good and true people.

Also, whatever you do, do not let the people of the globe think all Jamaicans are scammers. We are not all cut from the same cloth; hence death must do what they need to do to walk on land and TRULY CLEANSE JAMAICA AND RID JAMAICA OF THE WICKED AND EVIL PEOPLE THAT ARE ON LAND.  Remember the wages of sin is death, and YOU LOVEY DID DEEM JAMAICA UNCLEAN; THUS DEATH OWNS THE LAND.

I will not go into the land of Jamaica and plea for any BECAUSE YOU DID FORBID ME FROM GOING THERE.

I cannot go there because in truth, this land truly do not belong to you, it belongs to death.

JamaicaF remember. So who am I to stand in the way of death when it comes to their wicked and evil own?

No Jamaican can complain when death takes them because they did sin reckless and rude to have this. Someone committing suicide because they were robbed by crooked and deceitful Jamaicans. Thus this is not the first time I am coming to you about this Lovey. I've talked to you about this before, but this is the first time I am cussing out death reckless and rude for letting shit like this happen.

I know death has a job to do Lovey but come on now.

What right do we have to rob each other blind? Lovey, I don't know. Maybe I over love you in truth too much, but I need justice to be served now man come on now.

Lovey, I know we rob you of life but have I not cussed out people for you?

Have I not called their gods stink?

No don't laugh Lovey. You know mi a tegareg that cannot stand injustice.

Laade have mercy because in all I will put away for you Lovey; an anyone tek a penny from you, trust me hell would not be able to contain my fury. Wey mi gi yu an summady tek a penny from yu. Lovey mek mi stap because the sun and moon would turn blacker than anything known to man when I am done. No light would or could touch earth to my fury and anger and you know this. So duly warn humanity about me and my fury when it comes to you and what I truly give you unconditionally because wow. Let mi truly stop.

Wow Lovey let me truly stop because I truly don't sheg around when it comes to me and you and my more than unconditional and universal truth of you.

Trust me no one in your abode or hell could wane my anger; fury, thus let me truly keep my peace because not even you and your strength could contain me or stop me. My temper I've told you is worse than yours and you know this; thus I don't dick around when it comes to me and you and what I do for others.

I don't joke around when it comes to my truth and true love and you know this.

Life is worth it and I am glad you did not make me a politician because if I was the President of the United States AND SEEING WHAT JAMAICANS ARE DOING TO MY CITIZENS, I WOULD IMPOSE SANCTIONS ON JAMAICA.

I WOULD BAN MY CITIZENS FROM GOING THERE AND SENDING MONEY INTO THE LAND.

I WOULD ALSO SEND JAMAICA A BILL FOR EVERY CENT JAMAICANS ROBBED MY CITIZENS. AND IF JAMAICA CANNOT PAY, I WOULD DIVERT ALL LOANS GIVEN BY THE IMF TO JAMAICA TO THE UNITED STATES TO PAY BACK THE MONIES STOLEN FROM THE CITIZENS IN THAT LAND.

PLUS I WOULD CHARGE JAMAICA INTEREST FOR THIEVERY.

NO IMPORTS, NO EXPORTS. Trust me all that I get (buy) from Jamaica; I would go to Africa and other lands for (to buy).

No Lovey, they want to wreck my people with their fuckry, then let me show Jamaica who has and have the fucking bigger balls.

They want to come into America, pay your fucking debt to my people because visa fees are triple and quadrupled.

You want American goods, then fucking pay my levy; fucking thievery tax. You want to steal from my people then fucking see what I can and will do to you. My people should not have to commit suicide because of you.

My citizens work hard for what they have so why the fuck should you come and fuck them up by stealing their birthright; what they worked so fucking hard for for retirement. Fucking work for your own and if I find that my citizens were a part of this fucked up mess; I will take everything from them including family. Their family must work for me for way less than minimum wage until your debt is paid off. So if they have to shovel shit whist the city workers sit around and laugh at them, then so be it. You don't rob your own.

Your fucking own is your fucking own and you are to secure them.

You do not let someone else rob your own. It's like robbing you. You are all one blood because you are all Americans come on now.

Fair is fair.

You would not like the distress on you, so why let it happen to your own? That person's life is a part of your life whether you like it or not. ***Blood don't fucking kill blood come on now.***

Wake the fuck up and do better for your own.

Wow Lovey, because my spirit is boiling right now and I better stop.

I better fill this book with fillers because if I continue, I will get more brutal. So I had truly better calm myself down and let my anger truly wane.

I know what it's like to need Lovey.
I know what it's like to starve and or go hungry.
I know what it's like to save for your children and to have someone rape you of your efforts by making you lose it all.

In all some of us do, we try to build for our future and to have someone willfully take that from you is truly not right. Why should someone just come in and take all that you've built?

What wrong Lovey, what wrong, hence I cannot forgive my own for this. So truly take away from them come on now.

Look at how I am trying to build you Lovey and finding it so hard; difficult to build you.

Look at how hard I've tried with you and you've tried with me. What if someone was to just come and snatch me from you just like that?

How would you feel if I was suddenly taken from you?

Who would bug you like this?
Who would write like this for you and to you?

Who would plea to you for truth and justice?
Who would nag you and tell you they truly love you more than unconditionally?

Lovey I've battled you for the truth, who would replace me in this way? Do I not come to you with all except for in this book when it comes to my anger?

And in truth, I am coming to you in this book. Lovey, I know what it is like to lose it all you know this. I know the pain and agony. I am still feeling the pain and effects of this pain and agony. I have to raise my children alone and our readers know this and can read this in some of my other books.

Homelessness and poverty is truly dear to me amongst other things. Like I said above, I know what it's like to want; be wanting of food, money, clothes, shoes, medicine. So no, it matters not to me who the person is; no one should rob them of life come on now.

Who feels it knows it. Thus I know it and I know the pain of being robbed come on now.

Look at my health woes and how my health and financial woes is robbing me of my life.

Do I not lash out at you from time to time about my health woes and financial hardship and pain?

Did I not tell you to get a job and help me?

So you too know.

Will I apologize for my anger in this book?

No, and I truly do not care if my own lash out at me. Nor do I care if other black people lash out at me for my angry thoughts and words.

NO ONE CAN JUSTIFY THEFT COME ON NOW.

We cannot say it's not me and I am not getting involved. Yes certain things you cannot get involved in but AFFAIRS OF THE HEART; YOUR TRUE HEART MATTERS AND IT DOES AFFECT YOU AND THIS AFFECT ME. LIKE I'VE SAID, I KNOW WHAT IT FEELS LIKE TO BE ROBBED; ROBBED OF LIFE.

No one should have to take their life because of another person's wrong and wrongs come on now.

I refuse to be an hypocrite when it comes to this come on now. I can't see wrong and not lash out in this way.

I lash out at other nations, what makes my own any different. Wrong is wrong because I am sure if the shoe was on the other foot, all hell break loose with the lay, lay.

Yes my spirit is waning and it's a good thing too.

So fuck you death; you're a nigga bitch and bitch nigga.

Grow some fucking balls if you can.


Michelle and Michelle Jean
October 08, 2015

So that is just some of the things I wrote yesterday in anger. And yes I know the black lash that is coming but so be it. I cannot be a hypocrite.

Many Jamaicans sing about the system but we can't just sing about the system. We have to rebel as Bob Marley said. _We cannot rebel with violence. We have to rebel in true peace and smarts._ And one way is to vote these political leaders out of office and vote in people that truly care about our country and people on a whole.

Leaders that will secure our future and not give it away.

You know how I feel about refugees. Like I said, we are the ones to vote demons and or wicked and evil people into political office and when they murder and kill us; we cry foul. What you vote into office is what you get. So truly think. Seek help from Lovey come on now. He will show you the good and true way come on now.

So yes this is my talk and who don't like it can bite it.

Michelle and Michelle Jean
October 09, 2015

## OTHER BOOKS BY MICHELLE JEAN

*Blackman Redemption – The Fall of Michelle Jean*
*Blackman Redemption – After the Fall Apology*
*Blackman Redemption – World Cry – Christine Lewis*
*Blackman Redemption*
*Blackman Redemption – The Rise and Fall of Jamaica*
*Blackman Redemption – The War of Israel*
*Blackman Redemption – The Way I Speak to God*
*Blackman Redemption – A Little Talk With Man*
*Blackman Redemption – The Den of Thieves*
*Blackman Redemption – The Death of Jamaica*
*Blackman Redemption – Happy Mother's Day*
*Blackman Redemption – The Death of Faith*
*Blackman Redemption – The War of Religion*
*Blackman Redemption – The Death of Russia*
*Blackman Redemption – The Truth*
*Blackman Redemption – Spiritual War*
*Blackman Redemption – The Youths*
*Blackman Redemption – Black Man Where Is Your God?*

*The New Book of Life*
*The New Book of Life – A Cry For The Children*
*The New Book of Life – Judgement*
*The New Book of Life – Love Bound*
*The New Book of Life – Me*
*The New Book of Life – Life*

*Just One of Those Days*
*Book Two – Just One of Those Days*
*Just One of Those Days – Book Three The Way I Feel*
*Just One of Those Days – Book Four*

*The Days I Am Weak*
*Crazy Thoughts – My Book of Sin*
*Broken*
*Ode to Mr. Dean Fraser*

*A Little Little Talk*
*A Little Little Talk – Book Two*

*Prayers*
*My Collective*
*A Little Talk/A Time For Fun and Play*
*Simple Poems*
*Behind The Scars*
*Songs of Praise And Love*

*Love Bound*
*Love Bound – Book Two*

*Dedication Unto My Kids*
*More Talk*
*Saving America From A Woman's Perspective*
*My Collective the Other Side of Me*
*My Collective the Dark Side of Me*
*A Blessed Day*
*Lose To Win*
*My Doubtful Days – Book One*

*My Little Talk With God*
*My Little Talk With God – Book Two*

*A Different Mood and World – Thinking*

*My Nagging Day*

*My Nagging Day – Book Two*
*Friday September 13, 2013*
*My True Love*
*It Would Be You*
*My Day*

*A Little Advice – Talk*
*1313, 2032, 2132 – The End of Man*
*Tata*

MICHELLE'S BOOK BLOG – BOOKS 1 – 22

*My Problem Day*
*A Better Way*
*Stay – Adultery and the Weight of Sin – Cleanliness*
*Message*

*Let's Talk*
*Lonely Days – Foundation*
*A Little Talk With Jamaica – As Long As I Live*
*Instructions For Death*
*My Lonely Thoughts*
*My Lonely Thoughts – Book Two*
*My Morning Talks – Prayers With God*
*What A Mess*
*My Little Book*
*A Little Word With You*
*My First Trip of 2015*
*Black Mother – Mama Africa*
*Islamic Thought*
*My California Trip January 2015*
*My True Devotion by Michelle – Michelle Jean*
*My Many Questions To God*

*My Talk*
*My Talk Book Two*
*My Talk Book Three – The Rise of Michelle Jean*
*My Talk Book Four*
*My Talk Book Five*
*My Talk Book Six*
*My Talk Book Seven*
*My Talk Book Eight – My Depression*
*My Talk Book Nine – Death*
*My Talk Book Ten – Wow*
*My Day – Book Two*
*My Talk Book Eleven – What About December?*
*Haven Hill*
*What About December – Book Two*
*My Talk Book Twelve – Summary and or Confusion*
*My Talk Book Thirteen*
*My Talk Book Fourteen – My Talk With God*